On the Road to the Cross

Leader Guide

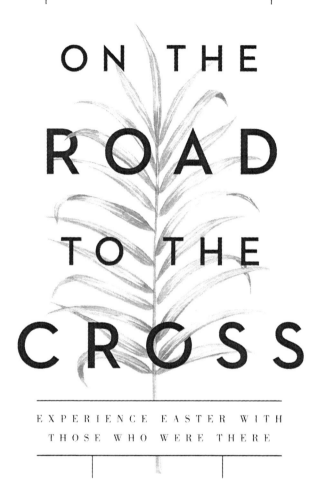

ROB BURKHART

ON THE
ROAD
TO THE
CROSS

EXPERIENCE EASTER WITH
THOSE WHO WERE THERE

Leader Guide

Abingdon Press
Nashville

ON THE ROAD TO THE CROSS
LEADER GUIDE

Copyright © 2016 by Robin Burkhart

ISBN: 978-1-5018-2267-4

16 17 18 19 20 21 22 23—10 9 8 7 6 5 4 3 2 1
MANUFACTURED IN THE UNITED STATES OF AMERICA

Contents

To The Leader

Easter is the turning point of human history and the turning point of our lives! Easter opens the door to eternity for anyone who believes its message and puts his or her faith in the resurrected Christ. Within that one great story are the stories of men and women who lived through those incredible days and witnessed a truth that is both unbelievable and undeniable.

The story of Easter is often told in the voices of its major characters: Christ, Peter, Herod, Pilate, and a few others. But the Gospel writers tell the stories of others who were in Jerusalem that week. Those lives are the subject of the book *On the Road to the Cross: Experiencing Easter with Those Who Were There* and this study.

The Study

This study is built around the stories of eight minor characters in the Easter narratives and focuses on issues or challenges common to all of us.

Character	Theme
1. Simon the Leper and the Sinful Woman	Inclusive vs. Exclusive Faith
2. Malchus, the High Priest's Servant	Overcoming Life's Wounds
3. The Centurion at the Cross	The War Within
4. Cleopas	Discovering Direction in Life

Character	Theme
5. Nicodemus and Joseph of Arimathea	Living Authentic Lives
6. Jesus, Barabbas, and Pilate	Finding True Freedom
7. Simon the Cyrene	Living an Engaged Life
8. Mary Magdalene	Dreaming after Disappointment

The study involves both the reflection and discussion of the scriptures and the author's insights. Participants should read the appropriate chapter in the book and the biblical material before the group session. If at all possible make copies of the book available to the group prior to the first session. Students should arrive with the book, their Bible, a notebook, and a pen or pencil. They should also arrive prepared to discuss the issues raised in the book and the scriptures.

Session Format

The sessions are designed to facilitate several important learning goals, foster growing relationships within the group, and build a sense of community. Group leaders should plan no less than 60 minutes and no more than 90 minutes for each session.

The design encourages the participants to discover the answers to four questions essential to a growing Christian life that focuses on changes in knowledge, understanding, attitude, and behavior.

What does the Bible say?

Participants should examine these stories for themselves and distinguish between what the scriptures say and the traditions and assumptions that have grown up around Easter.

What does the Bible mean?

Participants should discover principles, insights, and truths that may be new to them. The great value of the scriptures is found in the truths they teach not just in the stories they tell.

What does the Bible mean to *me*?

Participants should explore ways the Bible and its teachings are meaningful to them as they pursue the Christian life. Biblical truth has little or no value if it doesn't impact beliefs, attitudes, and lifestyle.

What am I going to do about it?

Participants are challenged to take action on their discoveries. Encountering truth should always result in a changed life.

Each session moves through the following steps to carry out the session goals in ways that lead to the discovery and application of biblical truth and a real-life response.

Getting Started

∽ Welcome Activity (5-10 minutes)

Participants rarely arrive at the same time, on time, or ready to get the most out of the experience even if they have read the scriptures and the chapter in the book. They are busy, dealing with the activities of their day and the stresses of life. The welcome activity accomplishes several important things. First, it ensures that learning begins when the participant arrives. Second, it helps participants focus on the learning experience. And third, it provides an opportunity for participants to interact, get to know one another, and build relationships.

Some group members may arrive after the time allotted for this activity. In such cases, skip this activity and ask them to join the group in what it is doing when they arrive.

The welcoming and learning activities in this study are intentionally simple and require a minimum of supplies or preparation. Leaders should feel free to replace or supplement the activities with those that may better serve their group.

∽ Opening Prayer (5 minutes)

Each session provides an opening prayer selected because it engages the theme of the session and helps participants focus on that theme. Group leaders should feel free to use the prayer provided or offer their own. True biblical learning depends on the presence of the Bible's author.

∽ Biblical Foundation (5 minutes)

A summary of the biblical material is provided as background to the scriptural exploration and provides a transition from informal interaction to intentional learning. Group leaders should not assume that participants are familiar with these characters or their stories. Taking a few minutes to provide that background and to focus on the theme of the session helps participants get more out of the biblical exploration and the discussion.

Learning Together

∽ Learning Activity (5–10 minutes)

The learning activity often builds on and uses the welcome activity. It allows participants to share their efforts, helps break the ice, and enables more open discussion and conversation. These activities are intended to be enjoyable. Group leaders should do all they can to make this portion of the study fun and lighthearted.

∽ Bible Study and Discussion (20–30 minutes)

Students are led to a firsthand exploration of the scriptures. While "second-hand" learning (listening to a sermon, reading a book, and so on) is valuable, it can only inform learners of what others have discovered. The most powerful learning is the result of personal discovery and active engagement with the material.

Six questions for discussion are provided in this section of the session in order to achieve three things. First, to identify what the participants discovered in the scripture. Second, to draw attention to the significance of those discoveries. Finally, to focus on the "big idea" or the main truth being taught in the story. Group leaders may, but need not, ask all the questions and may substitute questions that better serve their group. Or there may not be enough time to use all the questions. Leaders are, however, strongly encouraged to ask at least one question of each type.

～ Book Study and Discussion (10–20 minutes)

A few paragraphs from the book are reproduced to focus on the author's insights and conclusions. Group leaders may wish to substitute a different passage and modify the questions to better serve the needs of their group.

Four additional discussion questions are provided. These questions are intended to connect the biblical exploration with the book, encourage a critical evaluation of the author's perspective, and identify specific actions participants could take as individuals, a group, or a congregation as a result of the study.

Wrapping Up

～ Summary (3 minutes)

A summary statement is provided as a takeaway truth for the study. Group leaders should feel free to adapt or change the statement to better serve the needs of their group and to reflect their discussion.

～ Closing Prayer (5 minutes)

Each session provides a closing prayer that was selected because it picks up the session theme and helps participants commit to change and action as a result of the study. Group leaders should feel free to use the prayer provided or offer their own. All true biblical learning submits the results to the Bible's author and seeks his help in living a growing Christian life.

～ Headed Home (2 minutes)

Group leaders should take a few minutes to thank participants, remind them of the homework for the next session, and make any other announcements.

Getting the Most Out of This Study

The study can be used in a number of formats—an adult Sunday school class, a Bible study group, or a home group meeting. Most will teach one session each week for eight weeks during Lent. But it may be taught in fewer or more sessions depending on the needs of your learners. Pacing is critical. If you go too slow, participants will lose interest. If you go too quickly, they will be frustrated and may not get the full benefit of the study.

Regardless of the format, here are a few suggestions for getting the most out of the study.

1. Provide flexible seating that can be placed in a circle, a semicircle, or around tables.
2. Light snacks are always welcome and create a friendly, relaxed atmosphere that helps build the sense of community that is one of the goals for the study.
3. If there are more than a dozen participants, break the activities and discussion into smaller groups of no more than six to eight individuals. In such cases, allow a representative of each smaller group to report to the whole.
4. Be sure Bibles, copies of the book, notebooks, and pens or pencils are available to your participants in every session. Be sure you have enough supplies for the activities so all those who attend can fully participate.

Remember, the primary role of the group leader is to facilitate the learning experience and guide participants to discovering biblical truth for themselves. Your job isn't to tell them what you learned but to help them hear God's voice through his word.

Discussion Guidelines

Discussion is an excellent teaching tool to achieve the study's learning goals. It requires active engagement, careful thought, and the opportunity to learn from others. But not all discussion is "good discussion." The following guidelines will help your group maximize the benefits of this study. Remember that your role as the discussion leader is to ask questions clarifying participant responses, enforce the guidelines, and encourage more participation. Your role is not to lecture, dominate the discussion, or provide the "right" answer.

1. Create a climate conducive to discussion by assuring participants that they are valued, that their views are important, and that they will be treated with respect.
2. Encourage participants to listen carefully to what others have to say.
3. Don't allow participants to interrupt one another or to engage in "cross talk"—an interaction between two or more individuals that excludes the rest of the group.
4. Encourage group members to be honest and open with their views and thank them for their participation.
5. Encourage but don't demand participation by all members of your group.
6. Don't let any participant dominate the discussion. Encourage each person to let at least two other people talk before they speak again. Carefully and creatively deal with people who tend to take over the conversation. Your job as the group's leader is to make sure everyone has the opportunity to share.
7. Don't let the group wander off the topic. Monitor the discussion and interject a question or comment that refocuses the group on the session goals.
8. Affirm what others share even if their thoughts are different from yours or the group's. Affirm the person but don't endorse or approve of unbiblical perspectives.
9. If a participant's answer is unclear or seems incorrect, don't criticize. Ask him or her to clarify, tell the group more, or better explain his or her comments.
10. Encourage greater participation by asking group members to respond constructively (not critically) to what other participants have shared.

Helpful Suggestions

1. Provide plenty of get-acquainted time before and after the official start and end of the session. We all learn best among friends.

2. Begin on time even if some participants arrive late. The welcome activity allows everyone to participate when they arrive whether they arrive early, on time, or late.

3. End on time. Participants with other commitments can leave gracefully. Encourage those who can to interact after the official closing.

4. Pay close attention to the goals at the beginning of each session.

5. Begin and end each session with prayer.

6. Be sure those asked to read out loud are comfortable doing so and have advanced notice.

7. In several sessions ask participants to work in pairs or teams of three. People are more likely to participate with a few others than with the whole group.

8. Challenge people to interact with other participants and not just with their spouses, friends, or persons they know well.

9. Preparation matters. The more time you invest in reading, Bible study, and prayer before the session the more profitable the session will be for your group.

10. Trust the presence of the Holy Spirit to lead you and your group as you study his word. Remember, we are God's privileged partners but he alone can accomplish the great work of spiritual renewal and growth.

Session 1

The Leper and The Prostitute

Subject: Simon the Leper and the Sinful Woman

Texts: Matthew 26:6-15; Mark 14:1-11; Luke 7:36-50; and John 12:1-11

Session Focus: To examine the inclusive nature of true Christian life.

Session Goals: As a result of this session group members should be able to:

- explore the stories of the anointings of Jesus.
- identify and distinguish the characters in each story.
- examine the inclusive nature of Christ's response and its application to Christian life.
- contrast Christ's inclusive response with the exclusive response of the privileged and powerful.
- acknowledge the struggle to be inclusive and the temptation to exclude others.

- see themselves as both those who need Christ's inclusive grace and those who have suffered the pain of exclusion.
- apply Christ's model and teaching in their lives by the power and presence of the Holy Spirit.

Getting Started

∼ Welcome Activity (5-10 minutes)

Provide each participant with an index card or a half sheet of paper. Ask them to write their definition of *inclusion* on one side of the card and their definition of *exclusion* on the other. Encourage them to compare their definition with other participants as they arrive.

∼ Opening Prayer (5 Minutes)

As you prepare to discuss the joy of inclusive grace and the pain of exclusion ask the group to join you in this prayer written in the fourth century. Display it on a white board or print it on cards and distribute a copy to each participant.

O Lord and King,

grant me to see my own transgressions

and not to judge my brother,

for blessed art Thou unto ages of ages. Amen

—St. Ephraim the Syrian (AD 305–373)

∼ Biblical Foundation (5 minutes)

The stories of the anointing in Capernaum (Luke 7:36–50) and the anointing at Bethany (Matthew 26:6-15; Mark 14:1-11; and John 12:1-11) have long been confused and conflated since the time of Pope Gregory the Great (540–604 AD) who identified the sinful woman in Capernaum, the Mary who anointed Jesus at

Bethany, and Mary Magdalene as the same person. In a sermon on the Gospel of Luke, Gregory remarked: "This woman, whom Luke calls a sinner and John calls Mary, I think is the Mary from whom Mark reports that seven demons were cast out." Many still identify these three characters as the same person. A close look at the Gospels doesn't support that conclusion.

The anointing in Capernaum and the anointing in Bethany take place at different times in Christ's ministry, in different places, and with a different cast of characters. However, they both illustrate the same truths: the majesty of Christ's inclusive grace and the poverty of exclusive social structures.

Learning Together

∼ Learning Activity (5–10 minutes)

Ask volunteers to share their definitions of *inclusion* with the group. Ask, "How does it feel to be included especially if you are new to a group?"

Ask volunteers to share their definitions of *exclusion* with the group. Ask volunteers to share their experience of being excluded and how it felt.

∼ Bible Study and Discussion (20–30 minutes)

Ask four different participants to read each of the scripture passages. As they read, encourage the rest of the group to notice similarities and differences in each account. Remind them that the anointing in Luke occurred at a different time in Christ's ministry and at a different place than the other three. It tells a different story that teaches the same truth.

When the reading is complete discuss the following questions.

1. In what ways are the stories similar?
2. In what ways are the accounts different?
3. What different groups were present at the dinner? What divided them?
4. Why was the woman who anointed Jesus criticized?
5. Are there ways our times and culture are similar to these events?

6. What is the core truth Jesus is trying to communicate to his hearers and us?

∽ Book Study (10–20 minutes)

The author concludes this chapter with the following paragraphs.

There is no doubt: the impulse to exclude people exists today. Those who wish to be inclusive sometimes confuse loving and accepting people with approving of their behavior. They think that holding fast to a doctrine, a practice, or a lifestyle means excluding those who disagree or whose lifestyles they find offensive. It's a false dichotomy. We don't have to and shouldn't choose between loving and accepting people and living a lifestyle that honors God. Jesus loved people, led a sinless life, and never approved of or endorsed wrongdoing. We can and should do the same.

Easter belongs to everyone. Ethnicity, education, wealth, status, and power don't matter. Easter belongs to the ostracized and sinners, to the self-righteous and the religious, to the disinterested and the disheartened. It belongs to all of us because Jesus loves and welcomes all who come. It doesn't matter whether we come to worship, to question, or to struggle. All are welcome, just like the leper and the prostitute.

1. Do you agree or disagree with the author's conclusion? Why or why not?
2. How can the church maintain the truth of mankind's sin and need for a savior and still welcome those who are not yet believers?
3. How can we as individuals, as a group, and as a church welcome outsiders in ways that do not condone destructive lifestyles yet lovingly proclaim the gospel?
4. What steps do we need to take?

Wrapping Up

∽ Summary (3 minutes)

Easter belongs to everyone. It belongs to outcasts and sinners, to the self-righteous and the religious, to the disinterested and the disheartened. It belongs to us all because Jesus loves and welcomes all who come. It doesn't matter whether they come to worship, to question, or to struggle. It only matters that we come and follow Christ who gave himself for us. All are welcomed just like all were welcomed in Capernaum and Bethany—just like the leper and the prostitute.

∼ Closing Prayer (5 minutes)

As you prepare to end this session ask participants to share specific prayer requests. Encourage the group to note these requests and make them a part of their daily prayers. Then ask the person seated to the left of the person making the request to briefly pray for that person.

Finally, ask three volunteers to lead in prayer. Ask one volunteer to pray for their church as it reaches out to include new people. Ask a second volunteer to pray for healing for those who have suffered exclusion. Third, ask a volunteer to pray for the group to exercise Christlike inclusiveness in their personal lives.

Conclude your prayer time by leading the group in the following prayer:

Our savior,

you invite us to share in the glory of the resurrection.

Please stay with us as we struggle to see how accepting the crosses of our lives

free us from the power of the one who wants only

to destroy our love and trust in you.

Help us be humble and accepting like your son, Jesus.

We want to turn to you with the same trust he had in your love.

Save us, Lord. Only you can save us.

Amen

∼ Headed Home (2 minutes)

1. Remind the group of the next meeting time and place.
2. Assign homework.
3. Make any group "housekeeping" announcements.

Session 2

The Walking Wounded

Subject: Malchus the High Priest's Servant

Texts: Matthew 26:47-56; Mark 14:50; Luke 22:50-51; and John 18:1-10

Session Focus: To examine the healing power of Christ in hurting lives.

Session Goals: As a result of this session group members should be able to:

- explore the stories of Malchus, the High Priest's servant who was attacked by Peter.
- identify and distinguish the characters in each story—Malchus who was the victim, Peter who attacked him, and Jesus who healed.
- examine the power of Christ's work to heal body, mind, and soul, and access that power for their healing.
- contrast the way Christ responded to those who attacked him and the way people typically respond to such pain.

- acknowledge the challenge of dealing with those who harm them in a Christlike manner.
- see themselves as both victim and victimizer.
- apply the principles learned from this story to heal and make amends to those they have harmed.

Getting Started

∽ Welcome Activity (5–10 minutes)

Provide each participant with a craft wire (pipe cleaner, chenille wire) and ask him or her to think about the ways people are wounded and suffer today. Then ask them to bend their wire into a shape that represents that pain. Remind them that suffering may be physical, emotional, spiritual, mental, or relational. As other participants arrive, encourage them to greet one another and share their sculptures.

∽ Opening Prayer (5 minutes)

As you prepare to discuss the truth of Christ's power to heal our past pain, our present challenges and persistent struggles ask the group to join you in this prayer written by St. Ignatius of Loyola (1491–1556). Display it on a white board or print it on cards and distribute a copy to each participant.

O Christ Jesus,

when all is darkness and we feel our weakness and helplessness,

give us the sense of Your presence, Your love, and Your strength.

Help us to have perfect trust in Your protecting love

and Your strengthening power,

so that nothing may frighten or worry us,

for by living close to You, we shall see Your hand,

Your purpose, and Your will through all things.

Amen

—St. Ignatius of Loyola

∿ Biblical Foundation (5 Minutes)

The world is awash in the walking wounded.

On the great "take no prisoners" battlefields of life wander an army of walking wounded, who suffer mental, emotional, and spiritual wounds. Their wounds aren't always obvious but that doesn't mean they aren't real. Nor does it mean they suffer less. It only means others are not aware of their pain.

In this bizarre story, and even more bizarre moment, we are introduced to one of the Bible's walking wounded: Malchus.

We don't know much about him one way or the other. We know he was a servant of the high priest, probably a highly placed and trusted official. We know he was in the garden that night. We can guess from the story that he was leading or one of the leaders of the assault. After all he was at the front of the mob, standing close to Judas—within reach of Peter's sword and Christ's touch. Finally, we know he was painfully disfigured by a savage attack.

Learning Together

∿ Learning Activity (5-10 minutes)

Ask volunteers to share their sculptures with the group and explain what kind of pain it symbolizes and why they chose to craft that shape. When several have shared, explain that one of the most difficult parts of life is dealing with the painful wounds we suffer, and the results of those wounds in our lives and the lives of others. Ask volunteers to share ways or things that have helped them overcome their pain.

∿ Bible Study and Discussion (20-30 minutes)

Divide the participants into two groups. Make sure each group has a Bible, paper, and pens. Each group is to read the biblical stories found in Matthew 26:47-56; Mark 14:50; Luke 22:50-51; and John 18:1-10 and rewrite the narrative in their own words. Ask one group to tell the story from the perspective of Malchus the High Priest's servant and the other group to tell the story from Peter's perspective. (Allow 5–7 minutes for their work.)

Ask each group to read their story.

Discuss the following questions:

1. In what ways are Peter and Malchus alike?
2. In what ways are Peter and Malchus different?
3. Did either or both believe they were justified in their actions? Why?
4. In what ways do people harm one another today?
5. How do people justify their actions that harm others?
6. What is the great truth (truths) Jesus wanted Peter, his disciples, and us to learn from this story?

∼ Book Study (10-20 minutes)

The author makes the point that the power to heal is in the hands of the victim, other people, and ultimately God. He writes:

> That power is in the hands of the victim—but not the victim alone. Anyone standing there that night could have reached out to help Malchus. Maybe some tried. But none of them had the power to heal him. Only God could do that. We can comfort those in pain and be comforted in our pain. Such acts are magnificent and healing in and of themselves—no divinity required. But the miracle Malchus needed, and what so many long for, is beyond human ability. Fortunately for Malchus, Jesus was divine. Fortunately for all of us, he still is.

Ask:

1. Do you agree or disagree with the author's conclusions? Why or why not?
2. What steps do victims need to take to heal themselves and others?
3. What steps can those who have caused pain take to bring healing to themselves and their victim(s)?
4. What steps can we take as individuals, as a group, and as a church to be agents of Christ's healing power to those hurting in our family, our congregation, and the world?

Wrapping Up

∿ Summary (3 minutes)

All of us have been harmed and all of us need to be healed.

Any man standing in the garden that night could have reached out to comfort and help Malchus. Maybe some of them did. But none of them had the power to truly heal him. Only God could do that. So it is with us. We can comfort those in pain. Others can comfort us in our pain. We should. Such acts are magnificent and healing in their own right. No divinity required.

But the miracle Malchus needed and the miracle so many long for is beyond human ability. Divinity is most definitely required. Fortunately for Malchus, Jesus was divine. Fortunately for us, he still is.

∿ Closing Prayer (5 minutes)

Explain that we can still look to Christ for our emotional, spiritual, relational, and physical healing. All we need do is ask. Encourage each participant to share specific prayer requests focused on their own healing or the healing of another. Encourage the group to note these requests and make them a part of their daily prayers. Then ask the person seated to the right of the person making the request to briefly pray for that person.

Conclude your prayer time by leading the group in the following prayer:

Please Lord, sometimes our lives are a mess,

let your love flow through us and bring healing.

Let a river of cool refreshing water flow through us.

Not as a gentle stream or a rivulet of hope,

but a torrent, sweeping the debris away.

All those broken branches, our rust-encrusted past,

and the accumulated debris of our sins and failure,

which hold back the flow of Your grace.

Sweep them aside in a torrent of love, flooding through our veins,

pouring into our hearts, filling our lives.

This is healing. Thank you, Lord!

Amen

～ Headed Home (2 minutes)

1. Remind the group of the next meeting time and place.
2. Assign homework.
3. Make any group "housekeeping" announcements.

Session 3

When Worlds Collide

Subject: The Centurion at the Cross

Texts: Matthew 27:54; Mark 15:39; and Luke 23:47

Session Focus: To examine the internal struggle we face when the truth we know is at odds with the life we live.

Session Goals: As a result of this session group members should be able to:

- explore the stories of the crucifixion of Christ focusing on the role of the Roman Centurion and his men.
- identify and distinguish the characters in each story.
- examine the internal conflict people experience when they are confronted with a truth that does not align with their lifestyle or beliefs.
- contrast the nature of a life lived with such internal conflicts with one in harmony between belief and behavior.
- acknowledge that they too experience a "war within," especially when it comes to living a consistent Christian life.

- see themselves in the process of resolving these conflicts and being transformed into the image of Christ.
- apply the truths learned in this study to resolving their internal conflicts.

Getting Started

∾ Welcome Activity (5–10 minutes)

As participants arrive, provide each with an index card or a half-sheet of pape and ask them to complete the following statement, "Conflict is…"

When they've completed the statement, ask them to share and explain thei perspective on conflict with the other participants as they arrive.

∾ Opening Prayer (5 minutes)

We all struggle to live the life we hunger for and to overcome the brokennes of sin. As you prepare to discuss the hard reality of our internal struggle, ask th group to join you in this prayer written by German martyr Dietrich Bonhoeffe (1906–1945) who found himself in conflict with Hitler's Nazi regime. Display it o a white board or print it on cards and distribute a copy to each participant.

O God, early in the morning I cry to you.

Help me to pray and to concentrate my thoughts on you:

I cannot do this alone.

In me there is darkness, but with you there is light;

I am lonely, but you do not leave me;

I am feeble in heart, but with you there is help;

I am restless, but with you there is peace.

In me there is bitterness, but with you there is patience;

I do not understand your ways, but you know the way for me…

Restore me to liberty, and enable me to live now

That I may answer before you and before me.

Lord, whatever this day may bring, your name be praised.

Amen

—Dietrich Bonhoeffer

∿ Biblical Foundation (5 minutes)

A war rages in the depths of every soul. Most never find peace, only an uneasy armistice. A voice cries from beneath the calm surface that can be stilled but never silenced. A restless mind searches for a truth that is forever near and always just out of reach. The heart thirsts in the searing deserts of life and finds a mirage not the refreshing oasis of true love.

We are at war ... with ourselves.

Standing on Golgotha's hill a Roman centurion watched an innocent man die with dignity, courage, and honor. He had probably witnessed the ghoulish spectacle many times before, but he had never seen anything like this. The man dying on the center cross suffered like the others, but he dealt with his suffering like no other.

The Centurion saw it all, heard it all. But when Christ's head sagged in death, the Roman Centurion declared what was beyond dispute: "Surely, this was an innocent man, the son of God!" A great war between the life he lived and the truth he knew began.

Learning Together

∿ Learning Activity (5-10 minutes)

Ask volunteers to share their statement completions. Point out that conflict, while often thought of as negative, can also have positive results.

Ask: What positive results have you experienced or can we experience from conflict?

∽ Bible Study and Discussion (20–30 minutes)

Make sure participants have a blank sheet of paper and pens. Working in pairs, ask them to harmonize Matthew 27:54; Mark 15:39; and Luke 23:47 into a single statement. Allow a few minutes for their work and then ask volunteers to share their harmonies. Lead the group in a discussion by asking the following questions:

1. What conclusion(s) did the Roman Centurion reach about Jesus? How are they alike? How are they different?
2. What conflicts or potential conflicts did the Centurion's experience on Golgotha prompt in his life?
3. In what ways are the conflicts the Centurion faced similar to the conflicts people face in their lives and faith today?
4. What are areas of conflict that prevent people from accepting Christ and the message of the gospel?
5. How do people resolve such conflicts?
6. What is the great lesson we can learn from the story of the Centurion at the Cross?

∽ Book Study (10–20 minutes)

The author concludes his discussion of "The Centurion at the Cross" by stating:

Two worlds vie for everyone's heart, mind, and soul. One is the world we see, hear, touch, smell, and taste. Most live and die in and for that world.

The other world, the world of the Spirit, is just as real. But it is not necessarily the world of religion, even the Christian religion. Many religious people are firmly planted in the physical realm trying to gain favor with the divine by their righteous lives and religious practices—their own efforts.

People who truly encounter the realm of the Spirit begin to know God and his grace, love and forgiveness. His work, not ours, matters. He accomplished what we can never do. No wonder these worlds collide.

For a very brief moment the centurion peered into the other world. Then he disappeared. Perhaps he dismissed what he saw and went on with life. Most prefer the certainty of a world they can see to one taken on faith.

Others hope his story ended differently. I do. Perhaps that glimpse of glory turned him in a new direction and sent him searching for a greater truth. We'll know only in heaven.

In every life there is a moment when worlds collide. We catch a glimpse of glory and can choose to leave what we know and to live in a very different reality.

Some do. Most don't.

1. Do you agree with the author's conclusions? Why or why not?
2. What challenges or conflicts do believers face as they endeavor to live the Christian life?
3. What have you found helpful in resolving the challenges and conflicts you've faced living the Christian life?
4. How can we as individuals, as a group, or as a church help those who are struggling with coming to faith?

Wrapping Up

∼ Summary (3 minutes)

Every person has the same choice the Centurion had. In every life there is an opportunity to catch a glimpse of glory and choose to live differently and in a very different reality. But most people retreat into the certainty of what they know rather than risk it all on spiritual truth. Those who choose the world of the Spirit live with one foot firmly planted in both worlds and with a gaze that sees both sides. Believers are realistic about the fallen world they live in and take it seriously. But they live in a way that doesn't make sense to those who cannot see a greater truth and spiritual reality.

In *The Last Battle*, the final book in *The Chronicles of Narnia*, C. S. Lewis describes a moment when two worlds collide.

Rescued by Aslan the children look back on the dwarfs who could only see the shed in which they had all been imprisoned. While the door was open and the bright light of day shown in and a fresh breeze filled the shed the dwarfs remained trapped in their dark prison and its stench. The children begged Aslan to free them: "They have chosen cunning instead of belief. Their prison is only in their minds, yet they are in that prison; and so afraid of being taken in that they cannot be taken out."

Many live in such prisons.

∾ Closing Prayer (5 minutes)

As you prepare to end this session, ask participants to share specific prayer requests focused on those they know and love who are struggling with their faith. Ask them to give the person's first name and briefly explain the nature of their struggle. Encourage the group to note these requests and make them a part of their daily prayers. Then ask them to form smaller groups of three so that each person can pray for the other two.

Conclude your prayer time by leading the group in the following prayer:

Lord may today there be peace within.

May we trust You that we are exactly where we are meant to be.

May we not forget the infinite possibilities that are born of faith.

May all use those gifts that we have received from You,

and pass on the love that has been given to us.

May we be content knowing that we are children of God.

Let Your presence settle into our bones,

and allow our souls the freedom to sing, dance, praise, and love.

It is there for each and every one of us.

Amen

—Adapted from a blessing by St. Teresa of Avila (1515–1582)

∾ Headed Home (2 minutes)

1. Remind the group of the next meeting time and place.
2. Assign homework.
3. Make any group "housekeeping" announcements.

Session 4

On the Road to Discovery

Subject: The Two on the Road to Emmaus

Texts: Luke 24:13-35 and Mark 16:12-13

Session Focus: To examine the road to discovery of greater truth and integrity in our lives.

Session Goals: As a result of this session group members should be able to:

- explore the stories of Cleopas and his friend on the road to Emmaus.
- identify and distinguish the characters in each story: Cleopas, his friend, Jesus, and the disciples in Jerusalem.
- examine the experience of a life headed in the wrong direction.
- contrast failing to discover with discovering direction and meaning in life.
- acknowledge that all of us have taken the wrong path and needed to make corrections to discover meaning, integrity, and purpose.

- see themselves as travelers on their way to discovering more and more of his or her true identity as they pursue Christ.
- apply the lessons from this story to discovering in Christ the life they are meant to live.

Getting Started

∾ Welcome Activity (5-10 minutes)

As participants arrive, ask them to think of a time they were lost or had trouble finding their destination and to write the strongest emotion they felt at that time on a self-adhesive name tag or label, and attach that label to their clothes. Encourage them to share their experience and their emotion with other participants.

∾ Opening Prayer (5 minutes)

As you prepare to discuss the joy and challenges of discovering a life of meaning and purpose in Christ, ask the group to join you in this prayer. Display it on white board or print it on cards and distribute a copy to each participant.

Jesus, Lamb of God,
when you walked this earth
you did not consider heavenly equality,
though that was yours to choose,
but took the role of servant, and in humility
and obedience allowed the rough nails of our sin
to be hammered into your flesh
for the sake of our salvation.
Lord by the power of your love, grace, and mercy
enable your children to walk that road with you.
And so it is that we acknowledge you

as Lord of all, to the glory of God the Father,

Son and Spirit, Three in One.

Amen

∼ Biblical Foundation (5 minutes)

No one knows why Cleopas and his companion were on their way to Emmaus. We can only speculate. Perhaps they were just headed home. Maybe they were trying to get out of Jerusalem and Emmaus was close. We may never know why they were on the road, but we do know they got a lot more than they bargained for. They never expected an encounter with the resurrected Christ. In a very real sense they weren't just on the road to Emmaus.

They were on the road to a truly stunning discovery.

Cleopas and his companion weren't expecting to discover or encounter the resurrected Christ. But when that happened they discovered more than they ever thought they would. Everything they knew and understood about the meaning of life and their purpose in the world changed. They discovered a new reality and their place in it. That revelation changed the trajectory of their lives and its orbit.

Learning Together

∼ Learning Activity (5–10 minutes)

Ask for a volunteer to participate in an experiment. Explain that he or she will be blindfolded and asked to navigate around the room by listening to instructions from other members of the group. No one is permitted to touch the volunteer. Select a destination, blindfold the volunteer, and begin. Initially encourage all members of the group to call out instructions. Then select one person to verbally guide the volunteer. When he or she has successfully reached the destination ask the volunteer to return to the group and discuss this experience.

1. What made the experience hard?
2. What was most helpful?

3. What would have been helpful but wasn't offered?

◦ Bible Study and Discussion (20–30 minutes)

Ask a member of the group to read Luke 24:13-35 and Mark 16:12-13 aloud. As the participants listen, ask them to note important aspects of their journey such as:

- What led up to the journey?
- Where were they headed?
- Was it the wrong direction? Why or why not?
- What changed their destination?

Lead the group in a discussion by asking the following questions:

1. What made Cleopas and his companion believe they were headed in the right direction?
2. When people go off-track in their lives what leads them to believe they are headed in the right direction?
3. Why is it easy for people to chart the wrong course in life?
4. Why does it seem so difficult to follow the course laid out for us in scripture?
5. What helps us overcome the obstacles and find the right path for our lives?
6. What is the central truth the story of the two on the road to Emmaus teaches?

◦ Book Study: (10–20 minutes)

In reflecting on following the wrong path in life the author writes:

The companions' goal was a dusty little village seven miles away from the empty tomb. They missed the grandeur of the resurrection, the advent of the kingdom of God, and the inauguration of the church and its mission because they were looking somewhere else. Focused on what was in front of them, they could not see what was happening around them.

Some believe finding what their hearts most long for is impossible. It is a tragic self-fulfilling prophecy that bankrupts the soul. They never reach the goal, not because they can't but because they fail to factor in the divine. It is always a grave mistake.

1. Do you agree with the author's conclusion? Why or why not?
2. It's difficult to change course in life even when we know we need to. What are the obstacles to changing our direction in life?
3. What resources are available to us when we choose to follow Christ?
4. How can we as individuals, as a group, and as a church help one another choose and stay on a path that brings us ever closer to Christ and a full and rich life in him?

Wrapping Up

∽ Summary (3 minutes)

To discover ourselves we must discover the truth about our kind. We are beautiful and broken. Created in the image of God, we turned our back on him and his wisdom, will, and ways. We cannot truly know who we are until we know the One who created us and knew us before the beginning of time. Our identity is not so much discovered as it is revealed in the light of his presence.

We cannot know who we are until we know why we are here. We were created for a great purpose: to put on display his glory and reflect his likeness in the world. That is our great purpose. There are as many different ways to do that as there are individuals. No two of us are alike, but we all share his likeness and that great purpose.

Finally, we can only truly know ourselves when we know where we belong. We find our place in this world in his presence. We belong with him.

In their encounter with Christ, Cleopas and his companion were confronted with an incontrovertible truth that changed everything. They found themselves in him, in his call, and in his great mission. So can we.

∽ Closing Prayer (5 minutes)

As you prepare to end this session, ask participants to share specific prayer requests focused on those who are following the wrong road in life or are seeking God's direction. Ask them to give the person's first name and briefly explain the nature of their struggle. Encourage the group to note these requests and make them a part of their daily prayers. Then ask them to find a partner other than the person they came with and pray with and for their partner.

Conclude your prayer time by leading the group in the following prayer:

God you are our fortress in times of distress,

circling us in the safety of your arms,

granting peace when our lives are not at ease.

God you are our Father who knows us so well,

wanting only the best for your children,

willing always to forgive and forget.

God you are our refuge in times of trouble,

keeping our feet steady upon the road,

watching over us and keeping us from harm.

God keep us ever on the road of your love

so we may discover the riches of your grace and

true joy and meaning in life.

Amen

➳ Headed Home (2 minutes)

1. Remind the group of the next meeting time and place.
2. Assign homework.
3. Make any group "housekeeping" announcements.

Session 5

The Great Pretenders

Subjects: Nicodemus and Joseph of Arimathea

Texts: Matthew 27:57-61; Mark 15:42-47; Luke 23:50-56; and John 19:38-42

Session Focus: To explore the need for authenticity and the struggle to achieve it in our lives.

Session Goals: As a result of this session group members should be able to:

- explore the stories of Nicodemus and Joseph of Arimathea, especially their role in Christ's burial.
- identify and distinguish the characters in each story: Nicodemus, Joseph of Arimathea, and the Sanhedrin.
- examine the phenomena of pretending to be what we are not or of hiding from others what we truly are.
- contrast an authentic life lived in the open with a life lived in hiding and pretending;

- acknowledge that all of us are or have been guilty of hiding parts of our lives, sometimes with good reason.
- see themselves as needing to live with greater honesty and authenticity and helping others do the same.
- apply the principles learned in this story to better understand the struggle and overcome the barriers to authenticity.

Getting Started

∽ Welcome Activity (5-10 minutes)

As participants arrive, provide them with a sheet of blank paper and a pen. Ask them to find a partner other than the person they came with and create a list of things they have encountered or heard about that are "fake" or "pretend." They are to build a list as long as possible in the time allowed.

∽ Opening Prayer (5 minutes)

As you prepare to discuss the joy of an authentic life and the pain of a life lived hiding and pretending, ask the group to join you in this prayer. The prayer appears in the student study guide for this session, or you can display it on a white board or print it on cards and distribute a copy to each participant.

Father,
Your Word reveals to us a simple truth,
that sin entered this world through human folly
in believing we could be like you,
and permeated history through envy, selfishness, and greed.
Yet sin, which holds us tight within its grasp,
cannot resist a heart that is touched by your grace through Jesus Christ,
cannot contend with Living Water pouring into hearts and souls.

Your Word reveals to us a simple truth that sin is defeated and we can become

the people we were always meant to be, by your grace through Jesus Christ.

Amen

∾ Biblical Foundation (5 minutes)

"...in the world...not of the world."

These enigmatic words from Christ's prayer in the garden of Gethsemane (John 17) have plagued believers from that day to this. We are "not of this world" just as Christ was "not of this world." But, we are "in this world" just as he was in this world for a time. What does that mean anyway? Christ does not ask that his followers be taken from this world. Only that we be protected from the "evil one" and "sanctified" in it. In fact his followers are sent "into the world." Somehow we belong and don't belong to this world—at the same time.

How is it possible to be in culture, in place, and in time and fully participate in this life and not be "of the world"? Where are the "lines"? When does compromise become capitulation? How can we live a life worthy of the high calling of Jesus Christ and still "fit into" the world around us?

Many, like Nicodemus and Joseph of Arimathea, keep their faith quiet. They "pass," "blend in," pretend, or lead double lives of religious and spiritual chameleons. They aren't the first and certainly won't be the last.

Learning Together

∾ Learning Activity (5–10 minutes)

Ask the pairs to share the "pretend" list they created during the welcoming activity with the group. The object is to see who has the longest unique list. As each pair reads, the other pairs are to strike from the list any item that appears on another list. The pair with the longest unique list wins!

Point out that many things in life aren't genuine. But we all want the things and the people in our lives to be authentic. Being authentic isn't always easy.

᷍ Bible Study and Discussion (20-30 minutes)

Review the stories of Nicodemus and Joseph of Arimathea by asking a volunteer to read each of the following passages: Matthew 27:57-61; Mark 15:42-47; Luke 23:50-56; and John 19:38-42. Encourage other participants to follow along in their Bibles.

Lead the group in a discussion by asking the following questions:

1. Why weren't Nicodemus and Joseph of Arimathea open about their faith in Christ?
2. What prompted them to reveal their faith by offering to bury Christ?
3. Why do people pretend to be what they aren't and deny what they are?
4. What are the results of leading a "double life," of pretending to be what you are not, or of denying the person you are? For others in their lives?
5. Are there times when it's all right to pretend, to be less than completely authentic with what we think and feel?
6. What is the central truth we learn from the story of Nicodemus and Joseph of Arimathea?

᷍ Book Study (10-20 minutes)

In commenting on the challenge of living an authentic Christian life the author notes:

> It's no different today. Those open about their faith in Christ put themselves in harm's way. In some places a confession of faith means torture, prison, or martyrdom. In other places persecution means being overlooked for a promotion at work, losing a job, being denied admission to a school or university, or being rejected by family: disowned, divorced, or treated with great disdain.
>
> Dissatisfied with the lives they led, these men looked for something better, the kingdom of God. They were honorable men who struggled with a very real dilemma. They were chameleons with a conscience. Living double lives bothered them.

Honorable people may fail to live up to their own standards but not without the pangs of conscience, and not for very long. The dissonance is too loud. They abandon the deception or are destroyed by it. Some give up on their standards and redefine themselves. Others watch their souls rot, unwilling to resolve the tension. Some play the charade, destroy their consciences, and are concerned only when they get caught.

1. Do you agree with the author's conclusions? Why or why not?
2. What are the great rewards for living a more authentic Christian life?
3. What are the barriers to living a more authentic Christian life?
4. What can we as individuals, as a group, and as a church do to help one another live more authentic lives and be conformed to the image of Jesus?

Wrapping Up

⌒ Summary (3 minutes)

All who pursue an authentic life of faith, all who want to stop "passing" and pretending, face moments of great challenge and sacrifice. That fact is as inviolable as the sun rising in the east. There is no walk with Christ that is not also a struggle and a sacrificial walk. The gospel always has advanced and always will advance because brave men and women live truly authentic lives. They have great faith and willingly sacrifice what is of great value to them for the cause of Christ and to benefit those who do not yet know him. They are our examples and our heroes. They frighten us.

⌒ Closing Prayer (5 minutes)

As you prepare to end this session, ask participants to reflect on areas of their lives in which they struggle to live a truly authentic Christian life, are resisting God's call, or are unwilling to sacrifice for the cause of Christ. Ask them to observe a minute of silent prayer and bring their struggle to God.

Conclude your prayer time by leading the group in the following prayer:

Lord, grant us simplicity of faith
and a generosity of service that gives without counting cost.
Lord, grant us a life overflowing with Grace
poured out from the One who gave everything,
that we might show the power of love
to a broken world,
and share the truth from a living Word.
Lord, grant us simplicity of faith,
and a yearning to live it and share it.
Amen

∼ Headed Home (2 minutes)

1. Remind the group of the next meeting time and place.
2. Assign homework.
3. Make any group "housekeeping" announcements.

Session 6

The Great Exchange

Subject: Jesus Barabbas

Texts: Matthew 27:15-26; Mark 15:6-15; Luke 23:18-24; and John 18:38b-40

Session Focus: To explore the freedom found in Christ.

Session Goals: As a result of this session group members should be able to:

- explore the stories of Barabbas and the exchange that brought him freedom.
- identify and distinguish the characters in each story: Barabbas, Pilate, and Jesus.
- examine the nature of a truly free life.
- contrast the freedom found in Christ and the so-called freedom found pursuing our own desires and setting our own course.
- acknowledge that we all seek true freedom, that we all are in bondage to something, and that we cannot free others or ourselves.

- see themselves as struggling to find freedom and throw off the chains of the past, our pain, or the expectations of others.
- apply the principles learned in the story of Barabbas to discover true freedom for ourselves and help others discover it too.

Getting Started

∽ Welcome Activity (5–10 minutes)

Provide each participant with a half-sheet of paper with the word *free* written vertically along one edge. Ask participants to write as many words as they can that define or describe what freedom means and to begin with each letter of the word *free*.

∽ Opening Prayer (5 minutes)

As you prepare to discuss our need for true freedom that can only be found in Christ, ask the group to join you in this Lenten prayer. Display it on a white board or print it on cards and distribute a copy to each participant.

> *Father of light, in you is found no shadow of change*
> *but only the fullness of life and limitless truth.*
> *Open our hearts to the voice of your Word*
> *and free us from the original darkness that shadows our vision.*
> *Restore our sight that we may look upon your Son*
> *who calls us to repentance and a change of heart,*
> *for he lives and reigns with you and the Holy Spirit,*
> *one God, forever and ever.*
> *Amen*

∽ Biblical Foundation (5 minutes)

Freedom is a "worship word," meaning we put great emphasis on the word and the concept it represents. (This phrase comes from *Star Trek*, "The Omega Glory," first broadcast March 1, 1968.)

People everywhere always protect freedom when they have it and demand freedom when they don't. They resist confinement and physical restraint and reject external control, regulation, or interference in their lives and fiercely insist on the power to decide and do what they want. Freedom really is a worship word.

On the day Christ died the lives of three men—Barabbas, Pilate, and Jesus—crossed paths. Two of them were prisoners, one of them their warden. But only one of them lived a truly free life. In the great exchange of guilt for grace we find the source of true freedom and the power to walk that path.

Learning Together

∽ Learning Activity (5-10 minutes)

Ask participants to share their lists of words that define or describe what freedom means to them. Work around the group asking each person to share one word without repeating a word that has already been mentioned. Continue until all the words have been shared.

Point out that freedom is one of the greatest privileges we have but we all define it differently. Freedom is limited in many ways, but being free is important to every person.

∽ Bible Study and Discussion (20-30 minutes)

Read the accounts of the exchange of Christ for Barabbas found in the Gospels (Matthew 27:15-26; Mark 15:6-15; Luke 23:18-24; and John 18:38b-40). Point out that not all prisons have bars and locks. Some prisons are found in the heart, the mind, and the soul. Discuss the concept of finding true freedom by asking the following questions:

1. In what ways are each of the three major characters (Christ, Barabbas, and Pilate) prisoners or free?
2. What are the kinds of "prisons" people find themselves in today?
3. What keeps people in their emotional, spiritual, and relational "prisons"?

4. How do people attempt and fail to escape their emotional, spiritual, and relational "prisons"?
5. In what ways do some believe they are free when in fact they are not truly free?
6. What is the most important truth we can learn from the story of Barabbas?

∼ Book Study (10–20 minutes)

The author reflects on the nature and value of freedom as a God-given capacity not a moral quality and writes:

> Freedom does not guarantee its wise use. Some use freedom to create, contribute—to build lives and legacies, to bless and benefit. Others use freedom to destroy and demean, to take and terrorize, to steal and hoard. The misuse of freedom inevitably, predictably, and ultimately leads to the loss of freedom. Barabbas used his freedom without regard to the consequences and so lost it.
>
> Our deep need to be free raises great questions about the nature of freedom itself.
>
> Freedom is a capacity, not a moral category. It is a gift from our wise and loving God intended for our joy. But much of the misery people inflict on each other could be avoided if we weren't free to live outside God's boundaries. Surely the God who created heaven and earth, who created all reality, could have managed that. It would have been easier for him too. So why grant us freedom in the first place?

1. Do you agree with the author's conclusions? Why or why not?
2. Why do people trade away their freedoms?
3. What is the relationship between internal, spiritual freedom and external, physical freedom in the ways we live life?
4. How can we as individuals, as a group, and as a church help one another and those around us know and experience true freedom?

Wrapping Up

∾ Summary (3 minutes)

We too can only know freedom when we truly know ourselves. Our true self isn't the reflection we see in the mirrors others hold, in our experiences, or in what others say. Our true self can only be known in relation to the God who created us. We only really see ourselves when we look through "God eyes."

We can only be truly free when we know our place in the world and when we are in right relationship with the One who created us. Our struggle to belong ends when we know, ultimately and finally, that we do not belong to any other person, race, nation, or even to ourselves. We belong to God and we always will. Nothing and no one can separate us from him and his love—except us.

We can only be truly free when we know and give ourselves to the great purpose for which we were created. People do not exist to be born, make little people, grow old, and keep the bankers happy until we die. We were made to participate with the almighty creator of the universe in the great and glorious cause of reconciliation. We are the agents of healing between people and between people and their God. When we know that purpose, we are free to live according to its dictates without regard to the consequences.

We are only truly free when we know we are safe. The uncertainty and insecurity of this existence is unavoidable and undeniable. But we are safe. Not because our physical safety will never be threatened but because in the midst of loss and pain we know our lives are guided by the hand of an all wise, all powerful, and all loving Father. Nothing truly bad ever really happens to his children. The worst we can imagine—cruel martyrdom, a torturous disease, the loss of everything and everyone we hold dear—are circumstances under the control of the One who loves us most. They may happen. But we are safe—in him.

Finally, we are only truly free when we know the future is secure. The future in this life is notoriously uncertain and insecure. We cannot know or control it. But we can rest in the fact that God himself holds the rest of our days here and in the innumerable eons of immortality that follow. So, we are free. No one and nothing can take from us what God has promised. They can kill us. But they can't take our lives. We belong to God.

∼ Closing Prayer (5 minutes)

As you prepare to end this session, ask participants to reflect on the areas of their lives in which they are not truly free or to identify a person they know or love who is struggling with a past hurt, an addiction, or other life-controlling problem. Encourage each participant to share one item or person with the group. Ask each person to pray for the person seated on his or her left.

Conclude your prayer time by leading the group in the following prayer:

Sovereign Lord,
your love, poured into the heart of Jesus who endured the nails of our sin,
defeated death to rise again and causes our hearts to sing
Hallelujah!
Sovereign Lord,
your hand has touched the dry bones of our faith,
your Word has breathed new life where there was death,
your spirit raised us up from where we lay,
your love has brought us home and to your Cross,
and by your grace we stand forgiven and free forever. Hallelujah!
Amen

∼ Headed Home (2 minutes)

1. Remind the group of the next meeting time and place.
2. Assign homework.
3. Make any group "housekeeping" announcements.

Session 7

The Bystander

Subject: Simon from Cyrene

Texts: Matthew 27:30-32; Mark 15:19-21; and Luke 23:24-26

Session Focus: To examine the importance of fully engaging in our
life and calling.

Session Goals: As a result of this session group members should be
able to:

- explore the stories of Simon the Cyrene who carried Christ's cross
  to Golgotha.
- identify and distinguish the characters in each story: Simon, Jesus,
  the Roman soldier.
- examine the challenges and risks of fully engaging in life and
  God's call.
- contrast a fully engaged life with a life lived on the sidelines.
- acknowledge that we are tempted to live as bystanders and to not
  complicate our lives by engaging in God's greater call.

- see themselves as tempted to draw a small circle around their lives and to ignore the needs of others and the call of God.
- apply the principles found in this story to lead a more engaged life for our joy, the good we can do, and the glory of God.

Getting Started

∽ Welcome Activity (5–10 minutes)

Provide a copy of the following brief "case study" to participants as they arrive

Exiting a freeway, James comes upon a man holding a sign asking for money to buy food for his hungry family. James considers the situation and drives by without acknowledging the man or giving him anything.

Did he do the right thing? Why or why not?

Encourage participants to interact with others about their response.

∽ Opening Prayer (5 minutes)

As you prepare to discuss the joys of living fully engaged in your life and in God's call, ask the group to join you in this prayer. Display it on a white board or print it on cards and distribute a copy to each participant.

Forgive us, Father, when we get distracted from our task.
Forgive us those times when we try to be all things to all men,
and fail to be anything to anyone.
You were a man of suffering, acquainted with grief,
loved and despised in equal measure.
You understand humanity, you know our failings,
you love us despite the people that we are.
When we, like Peter, deny you by words, actions, or inaction, forgive us.

When we, like Judas, are tempted to follow a different path, forgive us.

When we, like those in the crowd, allow you to be crucified, forgive us.

Bring us to the foot of the Cross to stand next to the one who,

looking into your eyes, declared,

"Surely this is the Son of God."

Amen

∾ Biblical Foundation (5 minutes)

Children love to play "Simon Says." Players follow the leader's instruction as long as it begins with "Simon Says." If they fail to do what "Simon Says" or obey when "Simon" doesn't "say" they are "out." The "winner" is best at doing what "Simon says."

The little story of Simon from Cyrene is like that. In his experience, Simon "says" to all who listen carefully what can and should be done to follow Christ in the deepest and most meaningful ways—to stop being mere bystanders and embark on a great adventure.

In Simon's encounter with Christ we find clues that illuminate how believers can move from being "bystanders" to active participants in the greatest adventure of all time—God's unfolding work of redemption. Like Simon, we can stop being mere spectators watching great events and start engaging and experiencing those events. We can leave the well-worn and clearly marked path of the ordinary and follow the wild trail to the extraordinary.

Learning Together

∾ Learning Activity (5–10 minutes)

Ask participants to divide into two groups based on how they responded to the Welcoming Activity case study. One group should be made up of those who think James did the right things and the other made up of those who think he didn't.

Ask the groups to discuss their decision and select a representative to defend their position to the other group. Allow some back-and-forth dialogue between the two perspectives.

Explain that it isn't always easy to know when we should get involved and when we should remain bystanders. But all of us want to live active and engaged lives for our good, the good of others, and the glory of God.

∼ Bible Study and Discussion (20-30 minutes)

Divide the participants into three smaller groups and ask them to read through the accounts of Simon of Cyrene from the Gospels (Matthew 27:30-32; Mark 15:19-21; Luke 23:24-26). Ask them to look for things they didn't realize were part of the story or that surprise them. Let each group share their discoveries.

Lead a discussion by asking the following questions:

1. Why was Simon a bystander on that day? What kept him on the sidelines?
2. What keeps people on the sidelines of life, refusing to engage the world around them?
3. What did it cost Simon to get involved?
4. What risks and benefits do those who actively engage in life and ministry face if they leave the sidelines and get involved with Christ's great mission on earth?
5. What are the attractions or benefits of a life lived on the sidelines, of refusing to get involved with Christ's work in the world?
6. What is the great truth we can learn from Simon's experience?

∼ Book Study (10-20 minutes)

In his introduction to the discussion of Simon of Cyrene the author writes:

Nothing indicates Simon was a follower of Jesus or that he had any inter-est in the crucifixion of two thieves and a rabbi. Cyrene was a long way from Jerusalem and travel was difficult, dangerous, and expensive. Perhaps he was going to the temple to sacrifice, making his Passover pilgrimage, keeping a business appointment, sightseeing, or meeting friends. If a frus-trated Roman soldier had not singled him out, he would have watched the ghoulish spectacle pass, gone on about his business, and faded into histo-ry's dusty pages as just another unknown face in the crowd.

Most of the time we are spectators watching the great events of life. Wars are won or lost—most stare from the sidelines. Political candidates rise and fall—many don't vote. Great companies wax and wane. Monumental cultural shifts shake the foundations of society—most just try to keep their footing and go on about their business.

Like Simon, most of us lead our lives from the sidelines. Why? It contradicts some of our deepest desires. Perhaps there are some clues in Simon's story.

1. Do you agree with the author's conclusions? Why or why not?
2. How do the distractions of this life keep us from fully engaging in Christ's great mission?
3. Are there limits to our engagement? If so, what are they?
4. What can we do as individuals, as a group, and as a church to help one another and those around us live fuller lives that are more engaged in Christ's work in the world?

Wrapping Up

∽ Summary (3 minutes)

Simon the Cyrene was an outsider, a mere bystander who moved from the nameless, faceless crowd to become an active participant in the greatest story ever told.

Our circumstances aren't the same, of course. But the opportunity is. The irresistible truth of the crucified and resurrected savior of mankind moves relentlessly through the world. It is an unstoppable force! Most, even most believers are mere bystanders. At best, God's work in the world is a diversion from our routines. That great story plays out in the background of our daily lives but goes by largely unnoticed.

But it doesn't have to be that way. God has called us. God has gifted us. God gives us tremendous opportunities to do something great with our lives and make a real difference in the world. All we need to do is step into the story.

∼ Closing Prayer (5 minutes)

As you prepare to end this session ask participants to reflect on their level of engagement in the cause of Christ. Are they active participants or passive bystanders?

Conclude your prayer time by leading the group in the following prayer:

God of infinite love,

you shower us with limitless gifts in life.

In our every thought and action today

guide us to the bright and loving light of your kingdom.

Help us to be aware of the many ways you allow us

to share in your life so intimately today.

Thank you for the gifts you have placed in our lives.

Help us use those gifts to build your kingdom,

serve your people, and bring the truth of the gospel to a lost world.

Amen

∼ Headed Home (2 minutes)

1. Remind the group of the next meeting time and place.
2. Assign homework.
3. Make any group "housekeeping" announcements.

Session 8

The Death of Dreams

Subject: Mary Magdalene

Texts: Matthew 28:1-10; Mark 16:1-11; Luke 24:1-12; and John 20:1-18

Session Focus: To build, with God's help, a great life after great disappointment or failure.

Session Goals: As a result of this session group members should be able to:

- explore the stories of the resurrection of Jesus.
- identify and distinguish the characters in each story: Mary, the other women, Peter, John, and Jesus.
- examine the truth that disappointment or failure is an all-too-common experience.
- contrast the ways people handle disappointment or failure and the result of those choices.
- acknowledge that all of us have had or will experience the pain of disappointment or failure and must decide how we will respond.

- see themselves as able by the power and grace of Christ to overcome failure and build a life that honors God and is full of joy and meaning.
- apply the principles found in this story to overcome the debilitating nature of disappointment and failure and to help others in that process.

Getting Started

∿ Welcome Activity (5–10 minutes)

Provide each participant with a half-sheet of paper and ask him or her to complete the following statements:

When I was young my dream was to...

I didn't pursue my dreams because...

When they complete that, ask them to share their responses with at least two other participants.

∿ Opening Prayer (5 minutes)

As you prepare to discuss the challenges of surviving great disappointment and failure and the opportunity to build a joy-filled, God-honoring future, ask the group to join you in this prayer. Display it on a white board or print it on cards and distribute a copy to each participant.

Loving Father,
So many times we've turned away from you
and always you welcome us back.
Your mercy and love gives us confidence.
Thank you for the invitation to share, fast, and pray
so that you can form a new heart within us.

Your powerful compassion for our weaknesses

leads us to ask for mercy

and to await with great hope the Easter joy you share with us.

Amen

∿ Biblical Foundation (5 minutes)

We know almost nothing of Mary Magdalene before she suddenly appears in the Gospels. Nor do we know much about her day-to-day life while she and the other women followed Jesus as he taught and preached. She and the other women appear, but only in the background of the great drama that played out in the Judean hills and the shores of Galilee.

But we know Mary Magdalene stood at the foot of the cross and watched her dreams die.

She came a long way from the small, sleepy fishing village Magdala, and a life wracked by demonic possession. Jesus delivered her and she followed him on all the long dusty treks through the Judean hills and the shores of the Galilee, the scorching days and the chilly nights. She and the others had served him every way they could all the way to Jerusalem, Golgotha, and ultimately a garden tomb on history's most unbelievable day.

After all, he had given her and all his followers a reason to live and a future—a great hope and dream. He was their Messiah and they thought they knew what that meant. Then, in just a matter of a few hours, all of that was gone. He was gone.

What do we do when dreams die? How can we live when the very reason for life vanishes?

Learning Together

∿ Learning Activity (5-10 minutes)

Ask a volunteer to share their childhood dreams and why he or she didn't pursue them.

Point out that some of those dreams were unrealistic. We didn't really have the opportunity or ability to achieve them. Some of those dreams were replaced by better, more satisfying, and more important dreams that fuel the lives we have now.

We all let go of some dreams, but dreams are still important for all of us. We all need to hope and dream so we can make choices that shape a future we want to live in.

∾ Bible Study and Discussion (20–30 minutes)

Review the story of the women coming to prepare Christ's body for burial on that first Easter morning and Mary's encounter with the resurrected Christ by reading John 20:1-18. Discuss the importance of finding the future of our dreams by asking the following questions:

1. What dreams died with Christ on Good Friday? How do you think Mary felt?
2. What do people feel when a cherished dream or hope seems no longer possible? Why?
3. Why are dreams and hopes important in our lives?
4. How did that day change Mary's dreams and her future?
5. What has to change in our lives when we experience the death of a dream if we are to find a rich and fulfilling future?
6. What is the central truth we should learn from Mary's experience at the Tomb?

∾ Book Study (10–20 minutes)

The author suggests that the death of our dreams, despite the pain and disappointment, can lead to great dreams and a richer and more fulfilled life. He writes:

All who experience the death of a dream and discover a new and vibrant life end up glad the old dream died. The dream they live now is so much better. Others spend entire lifetimes wandering in the wastelands of dead dreams, mourning their losses. What's the secret? What makes the difference?

The Bible is full of stories of people whose dreams died but who still went on to live extraordinary and magnificent lives. Their dreams and circumstances were vastly different but a single thread runs through their stories: they let go of their dreams and lived in God's dreams for them.

Our best dreams are pale shadows of the great things God wants for us. That shouldn't surprise us. He created us. Our dreams reflect the passions and personalities he gave us. But dreams that are paltry and unworthy of his image must die if we are to encounter the wonders of his great dreams.

1. Do you agree with the author's conclusions? Why or why not?
2. Why do we struggle so hard to keep dreams alive?
3. Why is it so hard to let go of our dreams?
4. How can we as individuals, as a group, and as a church discover God's great dreams for our lives, live them, and experience the joys of that life for ourselves, those we love, and those we influence?

Wrapping Up

∾ Summary (3 minutes)

Mary spent the rest of her life giving shape to the hopes, dreams, and aspirations of her resurrected and living Messiah. One has to wonder if she looked back at their hopes before Golgotha amazed at how little she understood and the paltry, small, and unworthy nature of those dreams. Did she come to the conclusion that the best thing that ever happened to her happened on the worst day of her life?

Mary Magdalene disappears from scripture after she carried the good news of Christ's resurrection to his doubting, frightened, and desperate disciples. We don't know what happened to her. There are legends, speculations, and stories, but no true history. But we can be sure Mary fully engaged the great mission of the Lord she loved and served. Mary lived her greatest dreams until the day she died. Will we? It's up to us.

∾ Closing Prayer (5 minutes)

As you prepare to end this session, ask participants to reflect on their hopes and dreams for the future. Are they hanging on to a dream that they should let go of? Are they living God's dreams for their lives or their own?

Conclude your prayer time by leading the group in the following prayer:

O Lord, that we could begin this day in devout meditations,

in joy unspeakable, and in blessing and praising thee,

who has given us such good hope and everlasting consolation.

Lift up our minds above all these little things below,

which are apt to distract our thoughts;

and keep them above till our hearts are fully bent

to seek you every day,

in the way wherein Jesus hath gone before us.

Amen

John Wesley (1703–1791)

～ Headed Home (2 minutes)

Thank participants for being part of the study.

CPSIA information can be obtained
at www.ICGtesting.com
Printed in the USA
LVOW08s1216031116

511420LV00006BA/15/P